Learn Juggling

Published by Hinkler Books Pty Ltd
45–55 Fairchild Street
Heatherton Victoria 3202 Australia
www.hinkler.com.au

hinkler

Editor: Jaclyn Crupi
Cover design: Hinkler Design Studio
Prepress: Graphic Print Group
Typesetting: MPS Limited
Image on page 7 © Natursports / Shutterstock
Image on page 9 © Kenneth S. Thorkildsen / Shutterstock
Other photos © Shutterstock (www.shutterstock.com)

ISBN: 978 1 7436 3608 4

Printed and bound in China

CONTENTS

WHAT IS JUGGLING?

Juggling is all about throwing something in the air and catching it. Sounds simple, right? It can be, but the art of being a great juggler is to learn how to toss the items being juggled perfectly every time. Every. Single. Time.

Juggling involves keeping the items being juggled in constant motion. You cannot take your eyes off the ball. It's a skill that anybody can learn if they set their mind to it. It will just take time and practice.

There is a rhythm to juggling that this book will help you master. It will take some serious practice but it's worth the effort.

Did you know?

American Joe Salter completed a juggling triathlon and is the world record holder. He completed the triathlon in one hour and 57 minutes. He swam 400 metres while juggling three balls, rode 26 kilometres while juggling two balls in one hand and then completed a 6.5-kilometre run while juggling three balls.

HISTORY OF JUGGLING

The art of juggling is ancient. Juggling is thousands of years old. It has been traced to ancient Egyptian times, around 1900 BC. There are illustrations of women juggling balls from this time. In ancient Rome, jugglers threw round stones, torches and even shields. There is also archaeological evidence to suggest the ancient Greeks enjoyed juggling.

During the Middle Ages we know that jugglers performed in France and in England there were wandering theatrical and court performers.

In the 1700s, juggling became an important act in circuses. Travelling circuses were a source of entertainment at this time and helped popularise the art of juggling. Many circus clowns juggled as part of their act.

Today, there are juggling clubs in many cities and towns all around the world.

Did you know?

The International Juggling Association was founded in 1948. They held their first independent festival in 1948. Starting in 1969, the IJA held championship competitions for juggling.

GETTING STARTED

Regardless of your reason for wanting to learn to juggle, the first step is always the same. We all have to start somewhere!

There are three golden rules to follow before getting started:

1. Don't juggle anything breakable.
2. Don't juggle with sharp items.
3. Don't juggle anything that is alive.

If you can follow these three rules then you're off to a great start!

You will need a good space in which to learn and practise. Make sure you keep away from windows, light fittings, breakable items and pets. A good idea is to stand close to a table or bed. Dropped balls will be easier to pick up and you're more likely to keep your juggling within a certain space. Outdoors is another good option.

Juggling objects

We're going to teach you the principles of juggling using juggling balls. But as you progress, feel free to use other items such as scarves, clubs, canes or hoops.

JUGGLING STANCE

The best stance for juggling is to stand straight, with your feet shoulder-width apart. Your arms should hang easily at either side of your body.

Before going any further with the stance, or with juggling, relax! There is no way you are going to be able to juggle if you are tense. Shake your shoulders and wrists for a minute or so. Wear loose-fitting clothing so you are nice and comfortable.

Once you're relaxed and standing straight, bend your elbows so your forearms are straight out from your body. Now pull your elbows in tightly towards your waist and turn the palms of your hands up, keeping your fingers together.

Relax!

If you need help relaxing into your juggling stance, scrunch up both your shoulders as high as they will go. Hold this position tightly for 30 seconds. Release and let your shoulders drop. Feels good, doesn't it?

BEGINNER MOVES

Stand comfortably in your juggling stance
(see pages 10–11). Begin slowly moving your right
hand up and your left hand down at the same time.
Keep the movement small, just a few centimetres
for now.

UP AND DOWN

Pick up one of your juggling balls.
Cup it in the hand you usually
write with. If you're right-handed
this will be your right hand, left
hand for left-handed people. Make sure the ball is
cupped in your palm. You are not to hold it in your
fingers and it's not to rest on the tips of your fingers.
Keep your forearms out in front of you, but keep your
elbows tucked in to your sides.

Imagine two points in the air above you. One is above
your right hand and one is above your left hand.
Both are level with the top of your head or just a few
centimetres higher.

Toss the ball to the point above your throwing hand
and catch it with the same hand. Repeat this a few times
until it feels easy to do. Now, do it with your other hand.
Again, simply toss the ball to the point above your hand
and catch it with the same hand. This will feel harder
and more unnatural than it did with your other hand.

Keep throwing the ball and catching it with this hand until it feels comfortable.

HAND TO HAND

Now it's time for something a little harder.

1. Assume your juggling stance. Cup the ball in your hand.

2. Now, toss the ball across your body in a good arc to the point

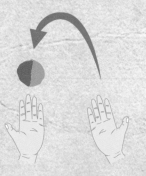

above your other hand. Catch the ball with your other hand.

3. Repeat in reverse.

Keep doing this movement for five or ten minutes. You need to get so comfortable with doing it that you can sway a little from side to side as you toss the bag from hand to hand.

When you're feeling really confident, try lifting your leg and tossing the ball under it. Catch it on the opposite side.

Spend as much time doing this as you need to. There is no point progressing to more difficult moves until you have mastered these.

Eyes on the ball

Your eyes are just as important as your hands when starting to learn to juggle. But you shouldn't only be watching the ball. You should also be looking at where you want to toss the ball. This will help ensure that you toss it perfectly.

TIPS AND TRICKS

These tips and tricks will help you perfect your moves and gain confidence with your juggling.

STANCE

If a movement is proving difficult to master make sure you haven't tensed your shoulders. Take a moment to make sure your shoulders are correctly placed, your legs are shoulder-width apart and your elbows are locked in at your sides.

Your stance is so important that you should stand in front of a mirror to make sure you're standing in the right way for juggling.

DROPPING?

If you are dropping more balls that you are catching, freeze your body after every drop. You need to check where your hands are. Are they right out in front of you or to your side? I bet your elbows are way out there, too. Work on your stance and that should improve your drop rate.

TOO HIGH?

If the ball is travelling way over your shoulder, you're throwing it too high. Keep the toss to the top of your head. Once you have the distance and the arc correct, the ball will fall into your hands every time.

LUNGING

Take a moment to check your legs and ensure they are shoulder-width apart. Have you stepped out of your stance to catch the ball? It's actually better to drop the ball than to lunge out for it – this teaches you bad habits that you should avoid.

If you are lunging out in front to catch the ball, you are tossing it forward instead of straight up. Keep practising the up-and-down throw and catch with just one hand to get this trajectory into your mind.

Eyes closed

A good way to know if you have a movement perfect is to close your eyes and see if you can still toss and catch the ball without seeing it. Juggling is about making the same toss every time so once you can do it, watching the ball becomes less important.

TWO-BALL JUGGLING

Now that you're comfortable with tossing and catching the ball it's time to progress to two-ball juggling! This is called the exchange or the two-ball cascade.

The aim is to move the two objects smoothly between your two hands using the scooping, arcing movement you have been practising with one ball. Adding another ball can cause a few problems, but don't worry, you'll get the hang of it.

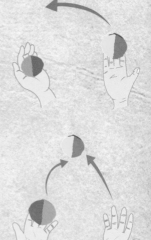

1. Hold a ball comfortably in the palm of each hand. Throw the ball in your writing hand gently up and across to the top point in the arc.

2. Just as this ball reaches its peak, throw the other ball underneath the first ball, up and across to the opposite top point.

3. Catch ball one.   4. Then catch ball two.

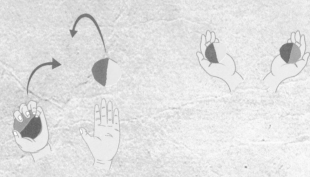

Easy, right? Perhaps not yet, but it soon will be.

Continue the cascade by immediately repeating the throwing and catching pattern until you are throwing the two balls continuously.

Rhythm counting

As you practise and practise this move you can count your way into a rhythm by saying one (as you throw), two (as you throw), three (as you catch), four (as you catch). Or just throw, throw, catch, catch.

TROUBLESHOOTING

Unless you are a totally naturally gifted juggler you will have had something go wrong with your first attempts at two-ball juggling. We'll review some common problems and show you how to fix them.

BALLS HITTING EACH OTHER?

Did the balls hit each other so you couldn't catch either one? The solution is to make sure you throw each ball on a different path – that is one on an arc inside the other.

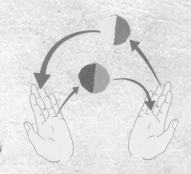

You also need to time your throws so that they are not happening at the same time. Remember to count or talk your way through – throw, throw, catch, catch.

BALLS HITTING THE FLOOR?

Are the balls hitting the floor before you've even said 'throw' the second time? It sounds as if you're not throwing each bag high enough to give you time to catch it. Remember that you need to throw up and over as well as reach that head height. You could try looking in a mirror as you throw but this doesn't work for everybody as it can be distracting.

Try kneeling on carpet and doing the throw. Don't catch the balls. Look down and see where they have landed. They should land in front of each of your knees. You may need to adjust your throws to make sure they land in front of your knees.

REACHING TO CATCH?

If you find you have to reach one way or the other to catch the ball, you need to go back to the basic throw. Up and down, up and down in one hand until you feel like that ball is on a piece of string. If you do this, you shouldn't need to step or lunge to catch the ball.

Take a break

When you've been practising for a while and nothing is going right or you don't feel you're improving, take a break. It will be easier when you come back to it after a break.

THREE-BALL JUGGLING

You've mastered the basics, now it's time for three-ball juggling. It probably won't feel natural to have three balls to juggle and only two hands. But, rest assured, there is a trick to it!

Until now you have only been using the palms of both hands. Now you will use your fingers for this third ball. Rest the third ball on your fingers, ready to let it fly. Start on whichever hand you feel more comfortable with using for two balls; this is usually your writing hand.

To keep both balls separate and to be able to control them, it's best to cradle the back ball with your pinkie finger and ring finger so it rests deep in your palm. Meanwhile, the front ball should rest lightly on the front of your palm held only by your other fingers and thumb. This third ball is the first one to be thrown.

It won't feel unnatural for long because apart from the beginning and your finale you will only have one ball in each hand at any one time. Most of the time, you will be tossing the balls in perfect arcs and catching them only long enough to toss them again.

THE EXCHANGE

This move is called the exchange. It just extends what you've already conquered with two balls.

Throw the first ball from your writing hand. When it reaches its peak, throw the single ball from your other hand. As soon as it reaches its peak, throw the remaining ball in your writing hand. Try to catch all the balls.

Did you catch all the balls? Any of them? Don't worry too much about catching them at this stage. Try focusing more on when to throw and the sequence of throws and less on how to catch the balls. Juggling is about timing.

Once again, throw the balls as described but don't try to catch them this time. Just let them fall to the ground. The balls should land near your feet on opposite sides from where they began. Work on getting this to happen.

Higher and higher

Once you are juggling the three-ball cascade through a few times you might find your hands rising higher and higher. Just be aware of this and bring your hands down again, level with your waist. Keep your elbows tucked.

THREE-BALL CASCADE VARIATIONS

Let's spice it up and add some variation to your three-ball cascades.

This first variation flies in the face of some of the technique you have had drilled into you. Just relax and go with it. You're expert enough now to be able to control it. Try varying the height of your throws. There are several ways to incorporate this trick into your repertoire.

HIGH AND LOW

First, throw all three balls quite a bit higher than normal – way over your head. This means that you won't be able to see all three bags at any one time. But if your throwing is accurate, you will have lots of time to throw and catch them. This variation looks great when done smoothly.

Now try to juggle the three balls really close to your hands by throwing much lower than normal. Your hands will need to move very quickly but you can always see the balls.

Finally, mix and match the heights you throw the balls for a cycle or two, high and then low. Keep it up for as long as you can. Keep the exchanges smooth as well as the turnover from high to low.

HIGHER

This next variation is a great performance piece. It is also the first step in many other tricks, so it's worth perfecting now. Juggle normally for a while. Start to occasionally throw one ball up much higher. Allow the ball to fall back and just before it reaches your catching hand, resume normal juggling. It will leave your audience in awe.

THREE-BALL CASCADE TRICKS

Have you practised and practised the three-ball cascade variations with alternate heights? Great! Here are four new tricks to learn.

JUGGLE WALK

Let's introduce a little walking. Get the cycle of the three-ball cascade moving and then, while keeping your back straight and your eyes focused somewhere near the top of your balls arc, move very slowly forward as you juggle. Start with three paces forward and then three paces back.

Trick extension
The next step beyond this trick is, of course, the juggle run!

JUGGLE SIT

Place a chair behind you. Begin juggling normally and once the cascade is flowing well continue to juggle and bend your knees until you are sitting. Make sure you use a solid chair that won't fall when you bang into it (which you will definitely do at the beginning).

Keep your back straight and watch the balls closely. Keep your tossing and catching under control. Now slowly stand up as you continue juggling.

Trick extension

Practice this trick until you can sit and stand any time you want to.

BLINDFOLDED

Juggling blindfolded is a great party trick. Have a quick juggle to make sure you are tossing and catching consistently and just to get the feel of it. Now place a blindfold over your eyes. Continue to juggle. Of course at first you may drop some balls or only catch one occasionally. This is a test of your accurate throwing so the better you toss the ball the easier this will be to accomplish.

Trick extension

Juggle blindfolded, while hopping! Good luck!

MUSIC

Juggle to loud dance music. You're trying to make a performance of your juggling and the music adds to it. Choose music to suit the pace at which you're comfortable juggling and just go for it. Incorporate high or low tosses when it suits the music. Sing along with the song for extra fun.

Trick extension

Dance juggle! Show us your moves while keeping the balls in the air.

ONE-HANDED JUGGLING TRICKS

Here are some new tricks to put up your sleeve. These will stretch you a little more in your juggling experience. They mostly all involve only using one hand which makes them sound deceptively easy. They're not!

TWO-BALL SHOWER

Pick up two balls – yep, just two. It may not sound tricky since you've mastered three-ball cascade but this is the trickiest trick so far.

1. Hold two balls in your writing hand. One should rest in your palm and the other on your fingers. Throw the ball on your fingers up and across to the left a little (assuming you are right-handed).

2. As the first ball reaches its peak, throw the second ball in the same way. If everything is going to plan, the first ball falls into your hand as the second peaks.

3. Keep catching and throwing, throwing and catching the balls in this way, creating a lovely circle of balls. Don't despair if it takes a while to get this right.

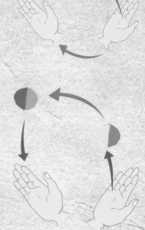

TWO-BALL COLUMN

Begin by holding both balls in your writing hand. Hold your fingers a little wider than normal. Toss the first ball straight up without any scooping motion.

As the ball rises, move your hand inside (to the left if you are using your right hand

and to the right if you are using your left hand) about 20 centimetres and as the first ball reaches its peak, throw the second ball straight up.

Quickly move your hand back to catch the first ball and throw it up again straight. In this move the balls are always thrown straight up with no scooping movement. They are not to cross each other.

Once you feel confident with both the shower and column tricks with your writing hand it's time to learn them with your other hand. Every good juggler can switch hands when they want to with these tricks.

Trick extension

Time your throws to achieve a good rhythm. After a bit of practice you'll be able to switch between the two-ball shower and the two-ball column.

THREE-BALL SHOWER

Yes, you can do these ball tricks with three balls in one hand.

Start as before with two bags in your writing hand. This time you also need a ball in your other hand. Begin doing the two-ball shower.

Once you are comfortable with the rhythm of the two balls in your writing hand, when you have just caught one of the balls, scoop throw it up and across to above your other hand.

When this ball is at its peak, throw the single ball in your non-writing hand up to the point above your other hand. You've worked yourself into the three-ball cascade.

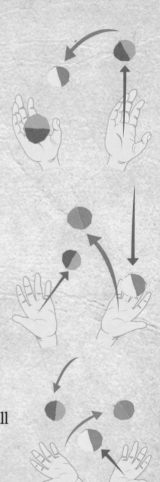

CHEAT MOVES

We've waited until now to tell you about these cheat ways to achieve some of the more difficult tricks you have hopefully already mastered. If you find the three-ball column hard to achieve here is the cheat move.

Begin by juggling the two balls in your writing hand and then, instead of throwing the ball in your other hand, just hold the ball in your other hand and move it up and down in time with one of the balls being juggled. Work on this until it looks completely smooth and real.

Another cheat move is the yo-yo cheat. Begin juggling a two-ball column with your writing hand, keeping it nice and low. Hold the cheat ball a little above the inside of the juggled ball and move the cheat ball up and down at the same speed as the thrown ball. The only hard part of this cheat move is the timing and making this trick look great by keeping the distance between the balls the same.

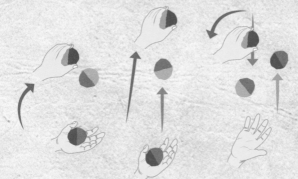

The real thing

These cheat moves are fun to do and can look really effective but there is nothing better than the real thing. Keep practising!

CLAWING

This trick is also known as the snatch. In this trick you actually juggle with your palms down. You need to learn this trick so you can perform it really quickly as that's how it looks most impressive.

Start with the one ball for now. Keep your palm down, holding the ball and use the scooping throw you know so well. This time though, you'll be doing it backhanded. Catch the ball by bringing your other hand down over it. Add in another ball until you can cascade three balls by clawing.

SCARF CLAWING

The grip of this trick is terrific if you'd like to try juggling with scarves. They look spectacular with their whooshing, flying colours. They're also slower than balls so it's easier to perfect this trick using them.

Begin with one scarf and perfect the one scarf cascade. The scooping throw motion is the same as always but this time you need to throw and catch palm down.

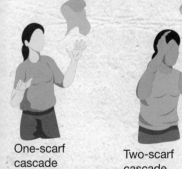

One-scarf
cascade

Two-scarf
cascade

Three-scarf cascade

Trick extension

If you want to take clawing further give it a try with your hands crossed. It's not easy!

BEGINNINGS AND ENDINGS

You can keep the balls in the air for as long as you like but what's most impressive is beginning and ending with a flourish. Every juggling routine needs a good start and an even greater finale.

ONE HAND START

1. Starting with three balls in one hand is super impressive. Place all three balls in your writing hand, two back in the palm and one balanced on your fingers.

2. Firstly just throw all three balls in the air together and don't worry about catching any. What you are trying to achieve is to throw the ball that began on your fingers, 30 centimetres higher than the other two.

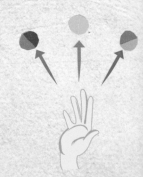

3. Once you've managed that it's time to catch the balls. You need to claw snatch the two low balls, so 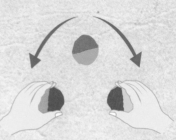 you'll be grabbing them out of the air with your palms down. Turn your hand over quickly and throw one back up in the air and catch the third ball. Throw it back up and juggle a three-ball cascade.

THE PUMP

This trick is also known as the greengrocer because it involves rolling the ball down your arm the way some greengrocers do with oranges or apples. It makes for a great start to a juggling trick.

1. Have two balls in your writing hand and one in your other hand.

2. Raise your writing hand forearm and roll the front ball backwards until it reaches the inside of your elbow.

3. Snap your arm straight and the ball should fly upwards through the air.

4. Treat this ball as the first ball of a three-ball cascade and you're away!

THE TWIST FINISH

This trick is as simple as it sounds. As you are about to finish your juggling act, throw one ball up considerably higher than normal and then spin around on the spot. Catch the ball and accept the applause.

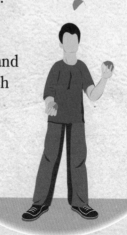

1. Throw one ball in the air really high and straight.

2. As it's rising, you should be already turning on the spot.

3. Once you've finished spinning and you're facing the front you have time to look up and catch the ball.

4. If you want to add a flourish, drop to one knee and bow to your audience.

THE NECK CATCH

This is a tricky ending but worth being able to do because it looks so impressive. Throw a ball high and as it falls, bend forward so your whole upper body is at a right angle. Now roll your head back a little and raise your arms out to the side. This creates a hollow on your neck. This hollow is where you need to catch the ball.

The secret to this ending is to keep moving down slightly as the ball hits your neck. This prevents it from bouncing straight off again.

MULTIPLE JUGGLERS

Juggling doesn't have to be a solitary past time. You can easily juggle with friends or family. Finding others who enjoy juggling can also help you to improve your technique as they might be able to give you some pointers or advice.

TWO-PERSON CASCADE

You will each only use one hand here. Stand side-by-side and link inside arms. Begin by tossing one ball back and forth in the usual scooping arc motion.

Now introduce another ball.

Once you're both comfortable introduce the third ball.

STEALING A BALL

This trick can be done from in front, to the side or behind the juggler.

1. Your partner juggles a three-ball cascade. Stand behind them and tap them on the shoulder.

2. This is the signal for them to continue juggling but drop to a kneeling position. Lean forward and steal the balls away as they are thrown.

3. Step back once you have three balls and continue juggling.

Trick extension

After you have 'stolen' the balls from your partner, they can crawl around behind you and start the trick again. Keep going for as long as you can.

NEXT LEVEL

So now that you're a ball-juggling master you want to take it to the next level.

The first thing you can do is start to juggle four balls at a time. That's two per hand to start. Then five, then six. There will be no stopping you!

You can also start to juggle different objects such as fruit and other household items. Just make sure that you can cup the item in your palm and you should be able to juggle with it (just make sure it's not sharp or dangerous).

Juggling is all about keeping things moving so keep learning and keep juggling!